A Tour of the Tabernacle

By
Barbara Ann Payne

PUBLISHING

A Tour of the Tabernacle

Copyright © 2022 Barbara Ann Payne

All rights reserved. No part of this publication may be reproduced, stored in a retrieval system, or transmitted in any form or by any means – for example, electronic, mechanical, photocopying, recording or any other – except for brief quotations in printed reviews – without the prior written permission of the author.

Scripture verses are mainly quoted from the New King James Version (NKJV)®. Copyright © 1982 by Thomas Nelson. Used by permission. All rights reserved.

Published in Great Britain by:

SelectArrow Ltd.
www.selectarrow.net

ISBN: 9798803708018

Cover illustration: Leo Francis
Interior design: Homer Slack
Editor: Angela Slack

DEDICATION

Dedicated to Pastor Jim and Joyce Sweet; who were fundamental in teaching me God's Word and inspiring me to search for Jesus in the Tabernacle.

ENDORSEMENT

This book, **A Tour of the Tabernacle,** will inspire you, as Barbara Payne, successfully unpacks this tour of discovery. **A Tour of the Tabernacle,** is a treasured jewel of God's redemption, an unveiling of Christ our blessed redeemer. It happened for me, and it will fill you too with a Holy Ghost excitement to explore this book and this journey. An exceptional book from an exceptional writer.

Well done, Barbara!

Pauline Hopes,
Intercessor.
Stoke On Trent, Lancaster,
UK

ENDORSEMENT

I want to say, thanks to the Lord Jesus for this book, **A Tour of the Tabernacle,** as the teaching is so clear and the pictures are so vividly described. Barbara Payne has a wonderful gift in the Holy Spirit of making scriptures understandable. She is a blessing to us all. Thank you Barbara for your clear insight into the word of God.

Lynda K. Smith
North East Lincolnshire,
UK.

FOREWORD

I have known Barbara Anne Payne, or several years now, and her love for the Lord and passion for His Word are abundantly evident in all she says and does. She has a deep longing to share the love for and knowledge of Jesus that she has with everyone she meets, and this is one of the approaches that she has chosen to help her fulfil this desire.

Throughout the book, **A Tour of the Tabernacle,** Barbara repeatedly backs-up everything with Scripture, quoting each Bible reference, and inspiring the reader to explore and study for themselves. She directs the lost to salvation and instructs the believer in the revelation she has received herself. Without over-simplifying, her target audience would include both new and mature believers alike, encouraging all to delve deeper into the meaning and understanding of what God reveals to us through His word.

Barbara Anne Payne, begins by giving an overview of what a Tabernacle is. She investigates its origin and history and describes its structure and purpose, detailing every element of this fascinating place.

She uncovers the journey the Israelites made with the Tabernacle when they were led through the desert by Moses. She explains who these people were, why they were making the journey, what happened along the way, where they were going and how the Tabernacle was such an important part of their survival and instruction in getting to know and worship their God.

She then goes on to describe the furnishings and objects used by the priests within the Tabernacle, highlighting their purpose and significance. Then she cleverly reveals each object's relevance to the plan of salvation and to the believer for today.

The book wonderfully reveals God's master-plan and takes the reader on a personal journey of discovery. It's a fascinating insight into how the Old Testament dovetails into the New Testament and it's my prayer that every reader will receive the revelation of Jesus that is to be discovered within the Tabernacle of God.

Pastor Trevor Nicklin.
Hanley Baptist Church,
Stoke on Trent,
UK.

PREFACE

The primary reason for writing about the Tabernacle of Moses is that I have been very disturbed over the years at how many Christians are unaware of its very existence, history, importance, and relevance in understanding our walk with Jesus Christ our Messiah. Some have been told that the Old Testament is not for them, they do not need to read it, etc… Oh my goodness! This is rife in the Church and it seems that unless there is a special teaching day about the subject or if it is a specialist subject for someone then most Christians do not understand the richness, significance, or even the necessity to understand the death and resurrection of Jesus, as it is set out in the Tabernacle. It sets out the order of worship that God Himself instructed Moses to teach the people of Israel. We learn how to become a temple keeper. We learn that we, in the present day, are the Temple of God and that we have a pattern of worship laid out in the Tabernacle of Moses that we need to not just know but apply to our lives.

Paul, the Apostle, wrote to the Corinthians who were non-Jews, *"... do you not know that your body is the temple [Tabernacle]of the Holy Spirit who is in you, whom you have from God, and you are not your own? For you were bought at a price; therefore glorify God in your body and in your spirit, which is God's."* 1 Corinthians 6:19-20 (New King James version) NKJV

The New is in the Old Concealed - The Old is in the New Revealed.

I have never forgotten that little gem of wisdom that my Pastor taught me. As we read the New Testament and it refers to the Old Testament it will give more insight and reveal a deeper meaning and understanding of what we read.

I have always loved reading about the deliverance of Israel and how God desired to dwell with His people. During my walk with the Lord, there was a realisation that the Tabernacle of Moses screams out, JESUS THE MESSIAH!

God has devoted over 40 chapters in His written word to the Tabernacle, more than any other subject. If we add to that the chapters on the priesthood and the sacrifices, along with the cloud by day and fire by night, it is clear God expects us to recognize the importance of studying these scriptures and having a clear understanding of how it applies in our day and generation.

"Moreover, brethren, I do not want you to be unaware that all our fathers were under the cloud, all passed through the sea, all were baptised into Moses in the cloud and in the sea, all ate the same spiritual food, and all drank the same spiritual drink. For they drank of that spiritual Rock that followed them, and that Rock was Christ but with most of them God was not well pleased, for their bodies were scattered in the wilderness.

Now, these things became our examples, to the intent that we should not lust after evil things as they also lusted. And do not become idolaters as were some of them. As it is written, 'The people sat down to eat and drink and rose up to play.' Nor let us commit sexual immorality, as some of them did, and in one day twenty-three thousand fell; nor let us tempt Christ, as some of them also tempted, and were destroyed by serpents; nor complain, as some of them also complained, and were destroyed by the destroyer. Now all these things happened to them as examples, and they were written for our admonition, upon which the ends of the ages have come." Corinthians 10:1-11

I pray that this book will help you to understand more of the Tabernacle and that you will be able to see Jesus in every part of it. It is God's assessment centre, of where we are in our journey with Jesus, how far we have come, and how much more we need to learn about our relationship with Him.

Every single part of the Tabernacle can be expounded upon but we are just going to go through the three courts and their furnishings and leave the curtains and skins and metal furnishings for another time or you can research them for yourself. Also, we will learn about the priesthood that was selected to serve God within the Tabernacle.

Ask the Holy Spirit to show you more as we walk through together, but you cannot study the Tabernacle without first recognising that as well as being the place of God's presence it is also a place of much blood. We will come to learn the reason for that as we journey together.

Enjoy and be blessed,

Barbara Ann Payne

CONTENTS

1. Background To The Tabernacle 1

2. The Outer Court 19

3. The Bronze Laver 33

4. The Holy Place 45

5. The Most Holy Place 57

xii A Tour of the Tabernacle

Chapter One

BACKGROUND TO THE TABERNACLE

Besides the tabernacle itself there is so much history of Israel that is unexplained. My aim here however, is not to explain all of Israel's history but to help you understand the Tabernacle a little better by examining it within the context of Israel's history.. The history of the nation of Israel started with Jacob whom God renamed Israel. **Genesis 32:28,** "And He said, 'Your name shall no longer be called Jacob, but Israel…'" Jacob's 12 sons then became the 12 tribes of Israel and the only people in the world chosen by God to be His people.

Due to a famine in the land Israel's sons went to Egypt to buy grain and eventually ended up living there for 400 years but whilst they were welcomed at first, as their population grew the Egyptians fearing their increased numbers, imprisoned and eventually enslaved them. They suffered abuse to the point of crying out to God to free them from this slavery. Egypt, at that time, was cosmopolitan and people from other countries would move there but they would also bring their false gods with them and so a culture of idolatry and many false gods grew and influenced Israel.

God eventually answered their cry and sent Moses as a deliverer to set the people free and you can read this exciting account in

2 A Tour of the Tabernacle

the book of Exodus. Unfortunately, living in a pagan culture of idolatry and many gods, Israel had forgotten the one true living God their ancestors had known and so He led them through the Wilderness of Sin, to purge them from Egypt's culture of idolatry and to teach them again how He was to be worshipped and revered.

This journey would normally be only 11 days but God led them around the same mountain for 40 years until they were ready to inherit the land that He had promised to give them, as only those who acknowledged Him and worshipped Him alone would enter. The Tabernacle was God's pattern for learning how to worship God on their journey. Paul the Apostle's letter in **1 Corinthians 10**, warns us to learn from what happened during Israel's journey through the wilderness. What are the vital lessons therefore to be learnt from the tabernacle?

Overview

What Is The Tabernacle Of Moses?

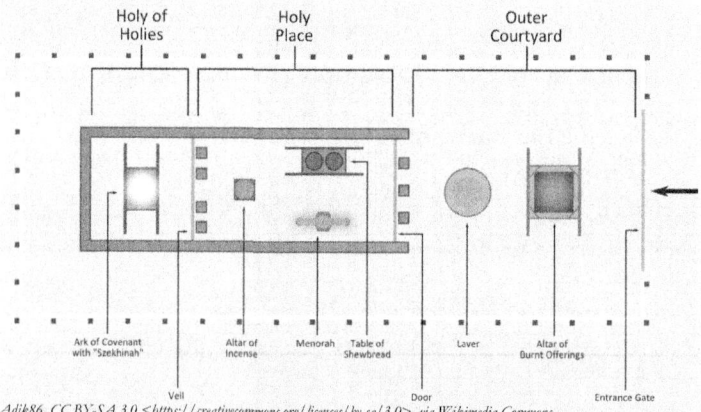

Adik86, CC BY-SA 3.0 <https://creativecommons.org/licenses/by-sa/3.0>, via Wikimedia Commons

Background to the Tabernacle

The meaning of Tabernacle is 'dwelling.' The Tabernacle is a dwelling place designed by God so that He could dwell amongst His people Israel. That has always been His desire from the book of Genesis until now and will never change. It is why God sent Jesus, so He can have intimacy with every human being He created who wants to know Him.

"And I heard a loud voice from heaven saying, "Behold, the tabernacle of God is with men, and He will dwell with them, and they shall be His people. God Himself will be with them and be their God." **Revelation 21:3**

The Tabernacle was a mobile tent so it could be transported from one place to another as the Israelites journeyed towards the Promised Land[1]. God went before it with a cloud of smoke by day and with a pillar of fire at night.

The pattern for the Tabernacle was not something God just made up, it was specifically built to be a replica of the one in heaven. It was designed by God and imparted to Moses during his 40 days on Mount Sinai with God, after the deliverance of Israel from Egypt. See Exodus 24.

However, you must remember that before this the Israelites had been in captivity in Egypt for over 400 years so where were they going to find the resources to build such an elaborate dwelling place (Tabernacle)? Also, who was going to build it? Let us take a look at **Exodus 11:1-3**.

---

1. God had promised Abraham that he would give him the area known as Canaan, at that time, as his inheritance to be occupied by all his descendants who would be innumerable.

4   A Tour of the Tabernacle

"When the Israelites left Egypt they were given many jewels, cloth animals etc. And the Lord said to Moses, 'I will bring one more plague on Pharaoh and on Egypt. Afterward he will let you go from here. When he lets you go, he will surely drive you out of here altogether. Speak now in the hearing of the people, and let every man ask from his neighbour and every woman from her neighbour, articles of silver and articles of gold.' And the Lord gave the people favour in the sight of the Egyptians. Moreover the man Moses was very great in the land of Egypt, in the sight of Pharaoh's servants and in the sight of the people."

You see, when they were released from slavery in Egypt, Israel was given all these spoils gold, silver, jewels, glass, animals, skins and fabric and much, much, more. All these things would come in handy when it was time to build the Tabernacle. God didn't just ensure that they had the right material but also put His Spirit on certain men to know how to build and craft the articles for the Tabernacle.

Offerings for the Sanctuary

"Then the Lord spoke to Moses, saying: 'Speak to the children of Israel, that they bring Me an offering. From everyone who gives it willingly with his heart you shall take My offering. And this is the offering which you shall take from them: gold, silver, and bronze; blue, purple, and scarlet thread, fine linen, and goats' hair; ram skins dyed red, badger skins, and acacia wood; oil for the light, and spices for the anointing oil and for the sweet incense; onyx stones, and stones to be set in the ephod and in the breastplate. And let them make Me a sanctuary, that I may dwell among them. According to all that I show you, that is, the pattern of the tabernacle and the pattern of all its furnishings, just so you shall make it.'" **Exodus 25:1-9**

Let your imagination run wild here with me as we ponder how it would feel having been in captivity all our lives with no riches or fine dresses, jewellery, or even a mirror. Little did they know that the Egyptians would give them all of their wonderful riches. Imagine soon after receiving these things in their hands having to give them to Moses for the building of the Tabernacle. Would you be able to let them go?

I have a lovely friend who taught me very early on in my walk with the Lord to "hold all things loosely you never know when God may want you to give them away." That was wonderful, wise advice, and little did the Israelites know that they were going to have to give up their valuable possessions too.

GOD'S DESIRE, GOD'S DESIGN, GOD'S INITIATIVE and GOD'S PROMISE
This earthly Tabernacle is just a picture for us of the true one that is in heaven, yes Heaven!

"But Christ came as High Priest of the good things to come, with the greater and more perfect tabernacle not made with hands, that is, not of this creation. Not with the blood of goats and calves, but with His own blood He entered the Most Holy Place once for all, having obtained eternal redemption."
Hebrews 9:11:13

Understand what the Bible is saying, that by looking at the earthly Tabernacle we can see into heaven itself. Even though it is just a picture, type or shadow, much can be learned about Jesus from studying the Tabernacle and it becomes a measure of where our relationship with Jesus is.

Paul the Apostle, explains it here, *"For if He [Jesus] were on earth, He would not be a priest, since there are priests who offer the gifts according to the law; who serve the copy and shadow of the heavenly things, as Moses was divinely instructed when he was about to make the tabernacle. For He said, "See that you make all things according to the pattern shown to you on the mountain."* **Hebrews 8:4-5**

You will note that God said, "ALL THINGS!" Also, John the Revelator, describes his vision of heaven which corroborates Pauls' claim and the account of Moses' instructions recorded in **Exodus 25.**

"And the temple of God was opened in heaven, and there was seen in His temple the ark of His testament: and there were lightnings, and voices, and thundering, and an earthquake, and great hail." **Revelation 11:19**

Exodus 25, is where we see Moses receiving instructions from the Lord on what to do and how to build the Tabernacle which would be the centre of the lives of the Hebrew people, as through it God would dwell in the midst of them. This Tabernacle is amazing. We are able to discover much about Jesus within it and through it and, believe it or not, much more about ourselves. It becomes like an assessment centre to measure our spiritual growth in Christ.

So we have established that Moses did receive specific instructions and dimensions for the Tabernacle and everything that had to be within it. This means that our pattern of worship is not something that is down to us to decide. God has established His own pattern for us to emulate.

"Have them make a sanctuary for me and I will dwell among them make this tabernacle and all its furnishings after the pattern I will show you."
Exodus 25:9

Some of the instructions were:
- Make it a specific size
- Use specific materials, wood, gold, silver, woven fabric, goat's hair etc.
- Only designated persons are to carry it along in the desert
- God would tell them when to move and when to be still
- God would inspire chosen persons to build and make the furnishings
- Only God's chosen priesthood could serve within it

Moses was obviously a good listener even at his old age of 80 years old, he remembered everything that the Lord had spoken to him. In **Exodus 25:21**, God said to place cherubim on the cover (mercy seat) and that He would provide a testimony to go inside the ark. What could that mean? All these things must have seemed strange to Moses but whether it did or not he obeyed the will of God and 1000's of years later we have the benefit of his experiences and a deeper understanding of Jesus the Messiah. We will look at the meaning of this later on, in **Chapter 4**.

The Priesthood

Before we go into the Tabernacle itself we need a little understanding of the Priesthood that was called by God to serve Him within it.

Why Was The Tribe Of Levi Anointed As Priests?

"All Scripture is God breathed and profitable for teaching reproof, correction and training in righteousness that the man of God may be thoroughly equipped for every good work. **2 Timothy 3:16**

So we have Paul writing to Timothy stating all scripture is profitable, that's why we have God's word but it also trains and sanctifies us."

In **Revelations 1:6,** *"He has made us to be a kingdom and priests to serve his God and Father."* **1 Peter 2: 9** says, *"but you are a chosen race, a Royal Priesthood, a Holy Nation, a people for God's own possession."*

Revelations 20: 6 *"but they will be Priests of God and of Christ and will reign with Him for a 1000 years."*

We are called to be a Kingdom of Priests. Well, how is that possible? How can we fulfil that call? What does it mean to us and to God? What does it entail? As you can appreciate, this is not an in - depth study but I pray you will listen to the Holy Spirit Who gives us revelation and be encouraged to look further for yourselves.

1 John: 2:27, says that the Holy Spirit "will lead us into ALL Truth" and He will, if we ask Him. Let us go back to our roots then and trace the history of the priesthood up to today.

Let us begin at **Genesis 29:34** and look at the Priests that were of the Levitical order. The Levitical priests were sons of Levi who was the third son of Jacob and Leah. (As a son of Jacob he was one of the 12 tribes of Israel) The name Levi means 'attached' or 'joined together' and we can see the significance of that by noting in scripture the important role the Priests had within the Tabernacle.

You would never think of the Tabernacle without the priesthood or the priesthood without the Tabernacle. They were joined together from the beginning in God's divine order of things which is based on the 'pattern of heaven'.

The priests usually started work at 20 years of age and retired at 50. Most of the work was really heavy lifting, of sheep and bulls, the dirty work of slaughtering the animal sacrifice, cleaning and keeping the Tabernacle exactly how God wanted it.

If we move to **Genesis 49:7** you will see that Jacob as he was dying pronounced blessings on his sons as was the custom but he did not pronounce a blessing on Levi, in fact, quite the opposite, **He Cursed him.** He said they would be scattered in Israel and dispersed… there was just no future for them, they were under a curse and you will see the reason for that curse in **Genesis 34**.

Levi's sister Dinah, had been defiled (raped) by Hamor the Hivite's son Shechem so Levi and his brother Simeon decided to take the law into their own hands by killing many of the Hivites to appease their sister Dinah. Consequently, Jacob wanted nothing more to do with his sons Levi and Simeon. They had brought disrepute on the family so he cast them out and his prophetic utterance over his sons came to pass.

When we encounter the tribe of Levi in **Exodus 32:26-29** however, (without going too far into this account) we see them redeemed from the curse because they were willing to obey God even though it was something very hard to do.

This chapter tells the story of Israel's behaviour whilst Moses was communing with God on Mount Sinai. God was engraving the 10 Commandments on tablets of stone that the Israelites were to follow. Meanwhile, back at the camp, the Israelites had coerced Aaron to make a golden calf so they could worship it, instead of God. In **verse 7** of this chapter the Lord said to Moses *"Go down for your people, whom you brought out of Egypt, are corrupt."* Even though they had seen the miraculous deliverance of God they were returning to their old ways of idolatry by wanting an idol 'god' to worship. On descending from the mountain, Moses was furious and threw down the very stones that the finger of God had written upon, breaking them in the process. After asking his brother Aaron to explain what was happening, here he was faced with A GOLDEN IDOL, he was even more furious.

"So he stood at the entrance to the camp and shouted, 'All of you who are on the Lord's side, come here and join me.' And all the Levites gathered around him.

Moses told them, 'This is what the Lord, the God of Israel, says: Each of you, take your swords and go back and forth from one end of the camp to the other. Kill everyone, even your brothers, friends, and neighbours.'

The Levites obeyed Moses' command, and about 3,000 people died that day. Then Moses told the Levites, "Today you have ordained yourselves for the service of the Lord, for you obeyed him even though it meant killing your own sons and brothers. Today you have earned a blessing."' **Exodus 32:26-29**

Who Is On The Lord's Side?
The only tribe mentioned that stood alongside Moses were the Levites, declaring their allegiance to God, and in **verse 26** we see their repentance and restoration from the curse of their father Israel/Jacob. That command from Moses to the tribe of Levi, must have been the most difficult one of his leadership as he gave them the order to slay the rest of their brethren who would not come over to the lord's side and they did it. This was a remarkable act of obedience.

The Amplified Version of Exodus 32:29 puts it so clearly…
"And Moses said [to the Levites, By your obedience to God's command] you have consecrated yourselves today [as priests] to the Lord, each man [at the cost of being] against his own son and his own brother, that the Lord may restore and bestow His blessing upon you this day."

The Levites were now free from the curse of their father Jacob and became attached or joined to God. They were the only tribe to repent and so God honoured them with the priesthood, they would be the closest of tribes to God by serving Him in the Tabernacle throughout their journey. He had put His trust in

12 A Tour of the Tabernacle

them to be obedient.

This is where we see God in the restoration business; He restores the blessings which were lost by their forefathers. What a wonderful picture of God's plan of salvation! It is by these acts of **Repentance, Obedience, and Holiness** that we are recognisable as Priests unto our God. This is written for our learning and it becomes clear that these acts lead to *"Training in Righteousness."* **(2 Timothy 3:16)**

In the beginning of this chapter, we saw in the book of Revelations that we are to be Priests unto our God. How can we get that into our hearts from God's word? *"I have given the Levites as a gift to Aaron (high priest) and to his sons from among Israel to perform the services of the sons of Israel at the tent of meeting* [Tabernacle]." **Numbers 8:19**

Verse 21: The Levites purified *themselves* from sin by repenting and obeying the Lord which in turn leads to holiness; and washed their clothes and Aaron presented them as a wave offering (one of the meanings of the wave is perfume) a sweet-smelling fragrance to God. Then Aaron, the High Priest, also made atonement for them to cleanse them and presented them to God as a wave offering.

FYI - Note, holiness means to be set apart for God's service.

The Lord Jesus Christ, is our High priest. God has called us out of the world and given us to Jesus in the same way He called the Levites out of Israel and gave them to Aaron to serve him… how wonderful!

In **John 17:6** our High Priest Jesus, prayed to the Heavenly Father saying, *"I manifested thy name unto the men whom thou gave ME out of the world."* As He did then for His disciples, the same applies to us today.

All Priests Were Levite's But All Levite's Were Not Priests.
There were many tasks to be carried out by the priests throughout their journey. The Tabernacle had to be taken down, carried and rebuilt in each new place that God led them to and this had to be done in the prescribed order and by appointed Levites.

Most people know this scripture very well, *"For God so loved the world that He gave His only Son that whosoever believes in Him shall not perish but have everlasting life."* **John 3:16**

We are all born into sin and corruption God said in **Genesis 6:5-7,** *"then the Lord saw that the wickedness of man was great in the earth and that every intent of the thoughts of his heart was only evil continually. And the Lord was sorry that He had made man on the earth, and He was grieved in His heart. So the Lord said, 'I will destroy man whom I have created from the face of the earth, man and beast, creeping things and birds of the air, for I am sorry that I have made them.' "*

When I first read that passage it really made me cry. God saw that we were corrupt and was even intent on destroying us BUT instead because of His wonderful love He sent His Son to die for us instead. Jesus made an everlasting atonement for us on the cross to cleanse us from all unrighteousness. We have to repent of our sin and disobedience and if we read and obey the Word of God this will lead us into righteousness. **Numbers 35**, gives us the picture of the Levites inheritance.

Once we were under a curse, because of sin, like Levi was cursed by his father BUT now, like the Levites, we have been chosen to be on the Lord's side. There are many mansions being prepared for us.

In **John 14** Jesus said, *"Let not your heart be troubled; you believe in God, believe also in Me. In My Father's house are many [a]mansions; if it were not so, I would have told you. I go to prepare a place for you. And if I go and prepare a place for you, I will come again and receive you to Myself; that where I am, there you may be also."*

We who follow Jesus Christ are His Priests here and now. We were given to Him because He bought us with His own blood and became the curse for us. *"You are not your own, you were bought with a price therefore glorify God in your body."* **1 Corinthians 6:20**

Just like at the foot of Mount Sinai when the Levites went over on the Lord's side so too we can go to the foot of the cross with the same attitude saying; we are on the Lord's side and partake in the inheritance that God has prepared for us.

We are called to be priests because we stand with our God protecting His sanctuary, ministering unto Him, and offering all kinds of prayers and supplications.

Praying and worshipping God has always been a priority, it started that way and it will continue that way in heaven **forever.** At this point I need to let you in on the meaning of a worshipper.

FYI: The word worshipper does not mean singer or singing; it means; reverence, respect, to reverently kiss, to move towards, and also TEMPLE KEEPER. WOW!

A true worshipper knows how to keep their temple (body). Paul the Apostle, tells us in **1 Corinthians 3:16**, "Do you not know that you are the **temple of** God and that the Spirit of God dwells in you?" We worship out of Love for our Saviour. Let us keep our temples undefiled so we can worship in Spirit and in truth.

As we begin our journey through the Tabernacle you will see beautiful furniture made from precious metals like gold, silver, and brass, and of course various models of the priesthood. God had gifted some artisans to make the priests' clothes and He put His spirit of wisdom upon these craftsmen. It is important that you take note that the clothes the Priests will be wearing are not all the same. A full description of their garments was given from the very start when Aaron, Moses' brother was called to be the High Priest along with his sons **(Exodus 28)** You will discover that Aaron's garments are very different and so also was His service to God. He was set apart. as the High Priest who alone was allowed to minister before the Ark of the Covenant in the

Most Holy Place. He made atonement on behalf of the people of Israel.

As you read the chapters of scripture relating to the consecration of the priesthood I want you to notice that in **Exodus 29:21** Aaron's garments were sprinkled not only with anointing oil but also with blood. Today, our High priest is Jesus and He was covered in blood on the cross. Moses was commanded by God to put on Aaron's garments; he did not put them on himself. All the garments Aaron had to wear were anointed, consecrated and put on him by Moses.

On his turban was a plate of pure gold with an engraving that read: 'HOLINESS TO THE LORD' which means 'set apart'. He had engraved onyx stones on his shoulders, six on each side; on them were inscribed the twelve tribes of Israel. I love the breastplate he had to wear that covered his heart, again with twelve precious stones representing the twelve tribes. He was dressed in costly gold, onyx, and precious jewels.

Note the similarities:
- Jesus was **covered in blood** as He died on the cross for the sin of the world.
- He was **anointed with the oil** of gladness **(Hebrews 1: 9)**
- He **carries the government** upon his shoulder **(Isaiah 9: 6)**
- Jesus is now seated at the right hand of the Father, as our High Priest, forever interceding for us. (The right hand is considered to be the place of honour, power and status throughout the biblical text.) Here are a few of these texts

that state that Jesus is seated at the right hand of the Father: **Hebrews 1:3, 12 :2, Peter 3:22, Act 7:55-56**
- He carries us in His heart *"I pray for them, I pray not for the world, but for them which thou hast given me;"* **John 17:9**

For the past 2,000 years since Jesus' resurrection, can you see the parallel between Aaron the High Priest and Jesus our High Priest today in the 21st century ?

The priesthood itself is a wonderful study on its own which I pray you may want to do. Get ready for an exciting journey and hopefully new revelations of the wonderful types and shadows of Jesus Christ, the Messiah that are found within the Tabernacle.

18 A Tour of the Tabernacle

Notes

Chapter Two

THE OUTER COURT

A PLACE OF SIN AND SALVATION

Sin is a Dirty Business!

Now let's begin our tour of the OUTER COURT. The Outer Court is 150 feet long by 75 feet wide and possibly 9 feet high. It is upheld by 56 pillars with sockets of brass. The curtain surrounding it is of fine twined linen representing the spotless righteousness of God. The height says 'no admittance' If you want to enter, you must find the GATE. This wonderful gate is 30 feet wide (again curtains) and all its colours of blue, purple, and scarlet speak of Christ. This is the only way into fellowship with God.

The wall of pure white linen represents God's perfect righteousness. The wide beautiful embroidered gate of colours speaks of the grace of God in Christ and says welcome come on in.

FYI - I want to give you some points to think about as we walk through the Tabernacle:
- Gold speaks of Deity
- Silver of Redemption
- Brass of Judgement
- Blue of Heavenly origin

A Tour of the Tabernacle

- Purple of Royalty
- Scarlet of Sacrifice
- Wood (acacia) of the Humanity of Christ
- Fine white linen of Righteousness
- Oil speaks of The Holy Spirit.

As we near the entrance to the Tabernacle, I want you to imagine that you are holding your innocent little lamb to be sacrificed for your sin. You begin to hear the cries and shrieks of other animals and see the tears of those who had brought their own animals for sacrifice, as they sloped back to their tents. Your animal, sensing danger, begins to shake in your arms through fear, and you are filled with guilt that this innocent little lamb will soon die for your sin.

FYI: You would bring your animal, make a confession to the priest, and then press hard on the head of the animal which **signifies transferring your sin to** the animal which is then slain for those sins.

As we draw back the curtain and look at the scene inside, the first thing that hits you is the smell. A horrible stench fills your nostrils because of the continuous slaughter and dead and burned carcasses offered to God for the forgiveness of the sin of Israel, **not the world you will note.** The sound of bleating sheep and frightened animals overwhelms you as you try to avert your eyes. Black smoke ascends daily so that everyone for miles around could see and witness the sins of Israel.

Daily sacrifices would be brought by each family, hoping that their offering of a lamb, goat, bird, or whatever animal that was available would be good enough for God to accept, to cleanse them from their sin. This was all new to Israel, they were still learning what this was all about but they acted in obedience to what God had told Moses was required of them.

Imagine that you are standing in the line of people waiting to give your offering, and you are finding it really hard to give this offering especially as you have developed a relationship with that animal and you didn't want to part with it. You are struggling with the reality that it was going to be killed, FOR YOUR SINS because according to the law almost all things are purified with blood.
"...and without the shedding of blood, there is no remission/forgiveness of sin." **Hebrews 9:22,** . This innocent animal's blood was being offered for you.

Here in the **The Outer Court** quite a few priests would be sacrificing animals. Some priests would be busy slaughtering and lifting animals onto the first piece of furniture that we see, the **Brazen Altar.** They are wearing blue robes and an ephod. The noise would be horrendous, with different animals screaming.

The Bronze Altar Of Sacrifice

The Bronze Altar is made of acacia wood overlaid with bronze. It is quite large, 5 cubits square and 3 cubits high and it has many types of utensils and a bowl in which to catch the blood of the sacrificial animal.

"Now the Lord called to Moses, and spoke to him from the tabernacle of meeting, saying, "Speak to the children of Israel and say to them: 'When any one of you brings an offering to the Lord, you shall bring your offering of the livestock of the herd and of the flock. If his offering is a burnt sacrifice of the herd, <u>let him offer a male without blemish;</u> he shall offer it of his own free will at the door of the tabernacle of meeting before the Lord. Then he shall put his hand on the head of the burnt offering, and it will be accepted on his behalf to make atonement for him. He shall kill the bull before the Lord; and the priests, Aaron's sons, shall bring the blood and sprinkle the blood all around on the altar that is by the door of the tabernacle of meeting.'" **Leviticus 1:1-5**

This is the cost of forgiveness, the shedding of blood, it demonstrates the cost of sin; The **Brazen Altar** showed the Israelites that the first step for sinful people to approach a Holy God and to be forgiven of their sin is to be redeemed by the blood of an innocent animal. In our passage above we read of how sin was transferred to the animal at the laying on of hands.

Can you imagine the emotions that would be running through your mind, knowing this had to happen. You would be doing this by choice and in faith. You first had to want to be reconciled to God and believe this was what was needed for your redemption.

This is where sin is atoned for through the shedding of the blood of an innocent animal. It is a hard, smelly, dirty, and painful job for the priest but God's mercy was also shown here. There were four horns on the corners of the altar that were used to tie the animal waiting to be sacrificed but these horns were also used by people who were falsely accused of murder. They could run there for safety and grab hold of one of these horns. If they were innocent they would be protected.

FYI: The Priesthood Worked Until They Were Fifty Years Of Age

The instructions from God in Leviticus on how to make the blood sacrifices to atone for the sins of the people of Israel (not the world) were very specific. See **Leviticus16 and 17**. God gave the reason He did this: *"For the life of the flesh is in the blood: and I have given it to you upon the altar to make an atonement for your souls: for it is the blood that makes an atonement for the soul."* **Leviticus 17:11** This was never about the animal, it was all about the blood of their animal.

It was a cycle of continuous slaughter day after day in obedience to God, and yet they would never see God or even come near to His Presence. There were 603,550 people of the tribes of Israel who **had no access to God.** Over half a million people who only knew that God was present because they could see the cloud of His glory that led them by day and the pillar of fire by night. Also they relied on the words of Moses and Aaron the High Priest.

I know someone who visited an abattoir many times and he told me how it affects you deeply and purges you the first time you see an animal being slaughtered. He said however, that after seeing it several times you can become hardened to the sight and therefore much less affected.

You see, it is all about the blood. Why? A Life required to redeem for a life and there is life in the blood and IT IS ONLY BLOOD THAT WILL APPEASE GOD FOR SIN and bring us back into a right relationship with Him.

The Garden of Eden

As we continue to look at why a blood sacrifice was required for Sin we need to go to the first book of the bible to get some background knowledge. **Genesis 2:7** says, *"And the Lord God formed man of the dust of the ground, and breathed into his nostrils the breath of life; and man became a living soul."*

Continue to read chapter three (I strongly suggest you read the whole chapter). You probably know most of the story of the fall of Adam and Eve but I want to draw your attention to **Genesis 3:7**, *"Then the eyes of both of them were opened and they knew that they were naked and they sewed fig leaves together and made themselves coverings."* **Note how they were immediately convicted.**

Back up to verse 25 of chapter 2 where it says: - *"And they were both naked the man and his wife AND WERE NOT ASHAMED"*. Before they were not ashamed but their disobedience (which is actually rebellion against God) came at a high price. They are now experiencing shame combined with a sense of guilt and fear. They were afraid to be seen by God so they hid from his presence. Why? They knew that He knew even though they had not said a word.

After God found them He pronounced judgement on them

and showed them that their OWN COVERING WAS NOT ACCEPTABLE. For adequate covering HE SLEW AN INNOCENT ANIMAL and used it's skin to make their garments **(Genesis 3:21)**. Consider the fact that the inside of the hide would have been covered in blood. This was the very first blood sacrifice. So yes, they had to take their punishment but God forgave them and took away the guilt, shame and fear. Most importantly, they had broken that wonderful communion they had with God in the beginning.

Here was the very first sacrifice for sin; the only type of sacrifice that would appease God. If we dig a bit deeper we will see in Genesis 4, that Cain, knowing his father's history had learned nothing, he too tried to bring a fruit offering to God but God did not respect it. Abel had obviously learned from his father's experience and brought the firstborn of his flock and the Lord respected Abel's offering.

Through jealousy Cain murdered his brother, *"And God said: what have you done? The voice of your brother's blood cries out to me from the ground."* **Genesis 4:10**

Sin affects our soul. It goes deep into us making our souls dirty and distressed. Those who are truly saved don't like sin and are very unsettled and uncomfortable with it. Trying to 'cover it up' will not help us or satisfy God. We can not draw near to Him with sin. God has provided a way for us to get rid of our sins and be reconciled to Him i.e. through the blood of Jesus our saviour.

"For the life of the flesh is in the blood: and I have given it to you upon the altar to make atonement for your souls: for it is the blood that makes atonement for the soul; not the body." **Leviticus 17:11** This is one of the most important passages of scripture. Remember what **Ezekiel 18:20** says? *"The soul that sinneth, it shall die."* These are God's words, precious words we should do our best to fully understand. We are a society that concentrates and puts a lot of emphasis upon the flesh. We attend the Gym to look good, carefully follow fashion and food fads and we do good works to make ourselves feel good. We tend not to even think about our own soul and its final destination but we most definitely should.

The soul has a destination and only we can determine where it ends up. Jesus tells the story of the sheep and the goats in the book of **Matthew 25:32-46** which should help us to assess our own lives very seriously.

In **Genesis 2**, God gave Adam and Eve a warning that if they ate from the tree of the knowledge of good and evil they would surely die. Guess what? They did and their souls died though they remained physically alive. I mentioned earlier that God slew an innocent animal to make a covering for them to indicate that the covering of sin required the shedding of blood. Fig leaves are inadequate. In time we also learnt that the animal used for the sacrifice must be without any blemish or flaw. To use a flawed animal was disobedience and rebellion against God.

Many today are using different methods to make themselves feel better; they do good works, they attend church regularly, they read and build up knowledge of the Bible and say things like, " I am a good person" hoping to please God, (these are the 'fig leaves' of today).

Only the blood of Jesus Christ can make atonement for our sins. We must believe it and demonstrate our belief by repenting of our sin and accepting Him as the unblemished Lamb of God whose sacrifice is sufficient to take away our sins. If we do this we will have that 'born again' experience Jesus spoke about in **John 3**. We must be 'born again' to see or enter the Kingdom of God. Oh, what joy this brings to the soul and what rejoicing takes place in heaven when one sinner comes to repentance. Oh, what peace! Oh, what love we experience from God Himself! The person who has this experience is no longer separated from God but is restored to a right relationship with Him through Jesus' sacrifice.

Passover

(Peshach in Hebrew)

When God delivered Israel from Egypt, He instructed the Hebrew slaves to kill a lamb and daub it's blood over the portals of the door and stay inside. When the Angel of death saw the blood he would Passover that dwelling. They were saved from death as long as they stayed inside the house under the blood of the lamb. Hence, the Jewish people still celebrate their deliverance each year. They call it Passover **(Exodus 12)**.

The process of killing that lamb and placing its blood over the doors and windows would include:
- Choosing a lamb without blemish and having it live with you

for 3 days (obedience).
- Sacrificing it.
- Catching its blood in a basin.
- Transferring/applying the blood from the basin to the door with a small weed known as hyssop that is very effective in doing such jobs.

When the Angel of death saw the blood he would pass over and not hurt anyone in the house. They were saved from death as long as they stayed inside the house under the blood of the lamb.

Listen to what Jesus says in **Matthew 26:28**, *"This is my blood of the new covenant which is shed for many for the remission of sins"* Paul the apostle repeats this in, **1 Corinthians 11:25**.

Today the blood of Jesus can be applied to anyone, not just Israel. The blood of Jesus will save from eternal death, anyone who applies it to themselves i.e. believe and accept the atoning work of Christ on the cross.

The Blood of Jesus

"Being in agony He prayed earnestly then His sweat became as great drops of blood falling to the ground." **Matthew 27 - 28**

FYI: This sounds like what doctors call hematidrosis. *"Hematidrosis is a condition in which capillary blood vessels that feed the sweat glands rupture, causing them to exude blood, occurring under conditions of extreme physical or emotional stress. It has been suggested that acute fear and extreme stress can* *cause hematidrosis." [1]*

We know Jesus was extremely stressed by what He was about to go through. He said, *"My soul is exceedingly sorrowful even unto death"* **Matthew 26:38**

- They struck Him and He bled.
- They pulled out His beard and He bled.
- He bled as the Romans whipped and scourged Him. The film, 'The Passion,' by Mel Gibson gives a very graphic view of what it may have been like for Jesus.
- When, in mockery, they put a crown of thorns on His head, He bled. The crown wasn't just placed on His head. It was pressed on causing the thorns to dig into His scalp resulting in blood running down His face. **Isaiah 52** says, "His visage marred more than any man."
- They nailed Him naked to a cross and eventually pierced His side to check if He was dead. This caused WATER AND BLOOD to flow out.

"He was despised, and we did not esteem Him. Surely He has borne our griefs and carried our sorrows; yet we esteemed Him stricken, smitten by God, and afflicted. But He was wounded for our transgressions, He was bruised for our iniquities; the chastisement for our peace was upon Him, and by His stripes, we are healed.

All we like sheep have gone astray; we have turned, everyone, to his own way; and the Lord has laid on Him the iniquity of us all. He was oppressed and

---

1. https://www.ncbi.nlm.nih.gov/pmc/articles/PMC3827523/#:~:text=Hematohidrosis%20also%20known%20as%20hematidrosis,or%20emotional%20stress.%5B1%5D

He was afflicted, yet He opened not His mouth; He was led as a lamb to the slaughter." **Isaiah 53:3-7**

Jesus' bleeding was followed by a victory cry, "It is finished!"
Jesus said, *"Do not think that I came to destroy the Law or the Prophets. I did not come to destroy but to fulfil."* **Matthew 5:17,** and when He hung on that cruel cross as a sacrifice of sin for the whole world, not just Israel, He cried, *"It is finished!"* He had completed the work of fulfilling the requirements of the law. The law required a sacrifice for sin and He fulfilled it once and for all.

I have often asked Christians what they thought Jesus meant by crying out those three most famous words. I have been rather startled at their reply. When Jesus cried "It is finished" He meant that His death has brought to an end all the sacrificing that took place in the Tabernacle/Temple. He accomplished once and for all the ultimate sacrifice for sin.

In my imagination, I see Jesus carrying His cross to Golgotha, 'the place of the skull.' In Jerusalem. He was bleeding and dying facing the cruellest death because of His love for you and me. He stumbles and as He glances over at the temple the priests are sacrificing the lambs at the yearly Passover feast, as it was during Passover that Jesus was crucified. He gazes with love and compassion for these priests, wanting to tell them that they no longer needed to perform that ceremony as He Himself was the *"Lamb of God who takes away the sins of the world."* **John 1:29** How sad, religion crucified Him, yet they still wanted their rituals and glorious temple; not a relationship with a Holy God.

As He cries, *"It is finished!"* Another important thing happened the veil of the temple** (the one that stands between the Holy of Holies where God's presence is) and the Holy Place, is torn in two. Now there is access to God, He has accepted His Son's blood for the whole world which includes you and me. His blood is crying out to God for you and for me. **The Father is saying to us, "the blood of my Son cries out mercy, for your soul!**

Hebrews 12:24, summarises it this way, *"Jesus the mediator of the new covenant, and to the blood of sprinkling, that speaks better things than that of Abel."*

1 Peter 1:18-19, reiterates, *"You were not bought with incorruptible things such as silver and gold but with the precious blood of Jesus."*

And again in, **Acts 20:28**, *"Take heed therefore unto yourselves, and to all the flock, over which the Holy Ghost hath made you overseers, to feed the church of God, which He hath purchased with His own blood."*

Based on these scriptures, we recognise that it is the soul of each one of us that is affected by SIN and the only way it can be redeemed is through the blood of Jesus whereby we are also reconciled to God. So now we are not ignorant any longer. Our journey has taken us from the garden to the Passover, then the Tabernacle up to the Cross.

We now have access to draw near **(Hebrews 10:19)** to God. Because of the blood sacrifice of Jesus Christ for my sins I am able to draw near to God, receive forgiveness and be reconciled to Him: to begin afresh having the right relationship with God.

You will know, when you read about the Brazen Altar, that it was a representation of the sacrificial death of Jesus Christ.

The New Is In The Old Concealed - The Old Is In The New Revealed.

Well, thank God He made a more excellent way for us to be forgiven and cleansed from our sin, with a blood transfusion (metaphorically speaking).

"For God so loved the world that He gave His only begotten Son that whoever believes in Him should not perish but have everlasting life." **John 3:16,** Let's pause and reflect and give God thanks for his wonderful provision of salvation through the blood of Jesus Christ.

Short Prayer:

Thank You Heavenly Father because of the blood of your Son Jesus Christ I am able to draw near to You, I now accept His blood sacrifice for my sin that enables me to be forgiven and reconciled to You: to begin afresh by having the right relationship with You.

** Solomon's Temple was built after the design of the Tabernacle.

Chapter Three

THE BRONZE LAVER

THE PLACE OF SANCTIFICATION

"He made the laver of bronze and its base of bronze, from the bronze mirrors of the serving women who assembled at the door of the tabernacle of meeting."
Exodus 38:8

As we leave the brazen altar we approach **The Bronze Laver**, or basin, where the priests would go after the ceremonial slaughter of animals and before they could enter the Inner Court or Holy Place, the place of service. The Bronze Laver was a large bowl filled with water located halfway between the brazen altar and the Holy Place. Although God did not give specific measurements for the Laver, it was to be made entirely of bronze and inlaid with the mirrors the women had brought with them from Egypt. This way they could see if any blood was left on themselves as the priests were to wash their hands and their feet in it before entering the Holy Place.

The Laver was located in a convenient place for washing *(see diagram on page 2)* and stood as a reminder that people need cleansing before approaching God. The priests atoned for their sins through a sacrifice at The Brazen Altar, but they cleansed themselves at The Bronze Laver before serving in The Holy

Place, so that they would be pure and not die before a Holy God **(Exodus 30:20-21)**.

The application for believers today is that we are forgiven through Christ's work on the cross, but we are washed and sanctified through His Word (the revelation of scriptures), and the Holy Spirit. We need to be washed daily in His Word to cleanse ourselves so that we can serve and minister before God. It is a physical picture of what happens to us when we go under the waters of baptism.

"Christ also loved the church, and gave Himself for it; that He might sanctify and cleanse it with the washing of water by the word. That He might present it to Himself a glorious church, not having spot, or wrinkle, or any such thing; but that it should be holy and without blemish." **Ephesians 5:25-27**

"Let us draw near to God with a sincere heart in full assurance of faith, having our hearts sprinkled [with blood] to cleanse us from a guilty conscience and having our bodies washed with pure water." **Hebrews 10:22 (NKJV**

"Therefore, because it was the Preparation Day, that the bodies should not remain on the cross on the Sabbath (for that Sabbath was a high day), the Jews asked Pilate that their legs might be broken, and that they might be taken away. Then the soldiers came and broke the legs of the first and of the other who was crucified with Him. But when they came to Jesus and saw that He was already dead, they did not break His legs. But one of the soldiers pierced His side with a spear, and immediately blood and water came out." **John 19:31-33 (NKJV**

What About The Holy Spirit?

The Bronze Laver can also be a foreshadow of or type of the Holy Spirit and our sanctification process cannot happen without Him. We fail to understand God's Word without Him. We cannot do it by ourselves. It is a divine-led, spiritual process in which God the Father through the regenerating power of the Holy Spirit sanctifies our souls. It is here we need to ask ourselves some questions and be brutally honest. Sometimes we deceive ourselves and are not honest but God's Word is like a mirror to our souls so when we read it, it reads us.

Maybe we can clear up some confusion over the baptism of the Holy Spirit.[1] **Romans 10:9-10**, is used by some to support the belief that you only need to acknowledge Jesus as your Saviour and you are automatically filled with the Holy Spirit.

"The word is near you, in your mouth and in your heart" (that is, the word of faith which we preach): that if you confess with your mouth the Lord Jesus and believe in your heart that God has raised Him from the dead, you will be saved. For with the heart one believes unto righteousness, and with the mouth, confession is made unto salvation." Romans 10:8 **This is a heart change, the salvation or conversion experience is being described here.**

This interpretation that you just have to believe, that's all, nothing else, and you will automatically receive the power of the Holy Spirit is inaccurate.

---
[1]. I have written a short book on The Holy Spirit which will explain much more about Him. 'The Holy Spirit' by Barbara Ann Payne - Available on Amazon.

On the other hand, Evangelicals and Pentecostals believe that you are only baptised with the power of the Holy Spirit if there is evidence of speaking in tongues (a heavenly language). This is a very controversial subject in Christendom. Not believing in Him however, does not make Him non existent. The Holy Spirit was given to the disciples in the upper room and all the other believers who were there with them.

Scripture gives us plenty of evidence to see that nothing happened in Jerusalem after the disciples saw Jesus in the upper room. Yes, they would have been overjoyed, but there was no power and they were still so afraid that Jesus had to appear to them again and again until they believed He was alive and had risen from the dead. They had to see Him!

After His suffering, He presented Himself to them and gave many convincing proofs that He was alive. He appeared to them over a period of forty days and spoke to them about the Kingdom of God. On one occasion, while He was eating with them, He gave them this command, *"do not leave Jerusalem but wait for the gift my Father promised, which you have heard Me speak about. For John baptised with water, but in a few days you will be baptised with the Holy Spirit."* **Acts 1:2-5 (NKJV**

John the Baptist said, *"I indeed baptise you with water unto repentance. But He that cometh after me is mightier than I, whose shoes I am not worthy to bear: He shall baptise you with the Holy Ghost, and with fire,"* **Matthew 3:11 and Luke 3:16** So, we see that there are three baptisms available to us to us. 1. We are baptised into water at our salvation/ 'born again' experience as a public show of our obedience and submission to the Lordship of Jesus Christ.

2. We are baptised into the Holy Spirit, also called the 'infilling' when Jesus Holy Spirit resides within us and instruct us in all truth.

3. The baptism of fire is an endowment/gift of power that gives us supernatural ability to serve God. It is followed by various marvels such as speaking in unknown languages, prophecy etc...

One night a man named Niccodemus went to Jesus to ask Him how could inherit the Kingdom of God and Jesus told him he must be 'born again.' Unless one is 'born again' he cannot see the Kingdom of God. What is born of flesh is flesh and that which is born of Spirit is Spirit. (**John 3:3**) Jesus' words are very clear and to be 'born again' means a regeneration of our spirit by God's Holy Spirt.

Personally, I have always wondered about Christians who say they are 'born again' and yet there is no evidence in their lives, nothing seems to have changed except maybe a point of view and belief. There is no demonstration of the Holy Spirit's power, and they seem to find it difficult to share their own testimony of how Jesus changed their lives. They believe by faith which is good but it becomes just a belief system that they have adopted and are quite happy that they have found Jesus and recognise Him as their Saviour. However, there is no visible change in their character and the fruit of their lives is not consistent with the fruit of the Holy Spirit.

"But the fruit of the Spirit is love, joy, peace, longsuffering, kindness, goodness, faithfulness, gentleness, self-control. Against such, there is no law."
Galatians 5:22-23 (NKJV

FYI: Saturday is the Hebrew Sabbath the last day of the week therefore Sunday in the Hebrew Calendar is the first day of the new week. Maybe looking at **Resurrection Sunday** and **Pentecost Sunday** will help us to understand more clearly.

First, let us look at **Resurrection Sunday,** with a view to understanding what is missing in the lives of many Christians. In this account, Jesus has been crucified and the disciples have hidden in an upper room terrified because now they are also guilty by association with Jesus. Jesus appears to them, and 'breathes' on them and says, *"Receive the Holy Spirit."* **John 20:19-22** They believed because THEY SAW HIM, twice and even touched Him, which is evidence that He had risen from the dead as He had promised.

The disciples had an amazing encounter with the RISEN CHRIST. Jesus showed Himself that He had defeated death, hell, and the grave, and we can have that same encounter, maybe not face to face as they did but an encounter it must be.

"If you confess with your mouth the Lord Jesus and believe in your heart that God raised Him from the dead you will be saved [born again]." **Romans 10:9 (NKJV**

The only way we can be 'born again' is through an encounter with Jesus. In John 3:3, Nicodemus had an encounter with Jesus, and those were the very words that Jesus spoke to him when he asked Jesus how he could save himself from God's judgement. Jesus said, "Ye must be born again." WE TOO MUST HAVE AN ENCOUNTER WITH JESUS. Have you been personally, 'born again' with the breath of the Holy Spirit (Ruah in Hebrew)?

In the Garden of Eden when God formed man He breathed into his nostrils and gave a dead body life or a living soul. It is our soul that is reconnected to God during the Baptism of the Holy Spirit. Just like connecting your mobile phone to its charger point; it gets filled with operating power.

In the account of John above, Jesus breathed on them and they knew Him but here the result **was life, the result was peace and hope, the result was joy instead of fear BUT NO POWER and a week later they were still hiding in the upper room. Jerusalem did not know anything about it as there was no evidence of power in their lives.** They were still afraid, Jerusalem was not affected by their experience at all. Everything stayed the same. Jesus even had to return to breathe on them again. That is to say, He returned to remind them of His word and strengthen their faith.

Luke 24:47- 49 In this chapter it was the women who went and told the disciples Jesus had risen and they didn't believe them! He eventually appears to them also and in **verse 49** He tells them to, "...wait until they are endued with power from on high."

In **Acts 1:4-5**, He tells them again, *"Wait for the promise of the Father' you shall be baptised not many days from now."* Also in **Verse 8**, *"but you shall receive power when the Holy Spirit has come upon you."*

I have personally been to 'waiting on' meetings where we prayed for the Holy Spirit to come upon us and be baptised, with all the right motives but not much happened. The Holy Spirit has already come so we no longer need to wait, we just need to sincerely hunger and thirst to be filled with His power.

Secondly, let us go to **Pentecost Sunday.**
Pentecost was the birth of the Church with fire and power and if we confess to having been baptised in the Holy Spirit we too should have that power to live for Jesus.

Here is the Ascended Christ, which fulfils what was prophesied as recorded in the Old Testament by the prophet **Joel in Chapter 2: 2**. A great outpouring of the Holy Spirit resulted in POWER FOR SERVICE (**Acts 2:1-12**).

Resurrection Sunday	Pentecostal Sunday
John 20:19-20	Luke 24:48-49. Acts 1:4-5
Resurrected Christ	Ascended (glorified) Christ
In-breathing of the Holy Spirit	Outpouring of the Holy Spirit
Result: New LIFE	Result: Supernatural POWER

Now let's look at the evidence of the outpouring of the Holy Spirit. Those upon whom the Holy Spirit was poured out increased greatly in courage, boldness resulting in a fearless preaching of the gospel causing many to come to know Jesus. **Now all Jerusalem**

witnessed the power of the risen Christ that was followed by the outpouring of the Holy Spirit. The evidence was seen with tongues of fire on people's heads. The evidence of speaking in new tongues is still around today. **Acts 2:14**

Read **Acts 8:14-17, 10:44** (Peter at Cornelius house) and **19:1-6.** This is an amazing act of God; the Gentiles at Cornelius' house spoke with other tongues and Peter was shocked to see that the promise of the Holy Spirit was not just for Jews but also for Gentile believers. The Apostles needed to realise that this gift of the Holy Spirit is now open to all who will receive Jesus Christ as Lord and Saviour Jew or Gentile.

There are many that say there is no more outpouring of the Holy Spirit; they argue that it all ended at Pentecost. Well, if that is so, who is building the Church today? Why did Jesus give the ministry gifts to men with the power of the Holy Spirit? I am convinced that we can have the same empowerment as those first disciples. It's the same Holy Spirit then as now. The scriptures prove that.

"The promise is unto you, and to your children, and to all that are afar off, even as many as the Lord our God shall call." **Acts 2:39**

It is for us today… Hallelujah! The baptism in the Holy Spirit is for service in the Kingdom of God and He gives gifts unto His Church for its building up and edification. Jesus speaking to the Samaritan woman by the well in **John 4:10-11** said, *"If you knew the gift of God, and who it is who says to you, 'Give Me a drink,' you would have asked Him, and He would have given you living water."* The woman *said to Him, "Sir, You have nothing to draw with, and the well is deep. Where then do you get that living water? Jesus replied, "He who believes in Me, as the Scripture has said, out of his heart will flow rivers of Living Water"*

The Baptism Of The Holy Spirit Is Distinctive

FYI: Mikveh or mikvah is a bath used for the purpose of ritual immersion in Judaism to achieve ritual purity. Most forms of ritual impurity can be purified through immersion in any natural collection of water. However, some impurities, require "living water", such as springs or groundwater wells. *Wikipedia* and you have to pay for it every time.[2]

When you go into the water you immerse yourself and come out soaking wet BUT during the baptism of the Holy Spirit He pours Himself into you and you give out of the overflow to others… out of your belly, rivers of living water (the Holy Spirit) flows **John 7:38**.

Most Christians are afraid of this experience so they never really ever achieve anything for God. They stay in **The Outer Court** all their Christian life working hard, getting their hands dirty, getting tired, never realising that they can draw even closer to God and enter into **The Holy Place**. They do everything in their own natural strength not in the power of the Holy Spirit or they say, "I am waiting for God to do it, if He wants me to have it He will

---

2. (https://en.wikipedia.org/wiki/Mikveh)

give it to me." Not so, there are also requirements from us and all we have to do is wash ourselves in the Word of God and receive the baptism of the Holy Spirit to be effective for service in the Kingdom.

So How Do We Receive Him?

"For every one that asks receives, and he that seeks finds and to him that knocks it shall be opened. If a son shall ask for bread of any of you that is a father, will he give him a stone? Or if he asks for a fish, will he for a fish give him a serpent? Or if he shall ask an egg, will he offer him a scorpion? If you then, being evil, know how to give good gifts to your children: how much more shall your heavenly Father give the Holy Spirit to them that ask him?" **Luke 11:11-13** .

"On the last day, that great day of the feast, Jesus stood and cried, saying, if any man thirst, let him come unto me, and drink. He that believeth on me, as the scripture hath said, out of his belly shall flow rivers of living water. But this spake He of the Spirit, which they that believe in Him should receive: for the Holy Ghost was not yet given; because that Jesus was not yet glorified." **John 7:37-39** .

If we ask the right thing in line with the Word of God we will get the right answer/response from God. So what do we need to do to receive this wonderful baptism?

- BE THIRSTY - that is, have a sincere desire and not be religious.
- COME TO THE BAPTISER - Jesus.
- RECEIVE BY FAITH His indwelling and let Him live in you.

We have an enemy, Satan, the same enemy that was in the Garden of Eden, that does not want you to receive the baptism. He will try to intimidate you with fear and many doubts. For example he will say: "You are doing this yourself… How do you know you have got the Spirit of God?"

Please note well, God will never make you do anything against your will, the Holy Spirit is a gentleman, not a force field to fear. Are you ready to receive? Are you thirsty? Are you 'born again'?

Here Is A Helpful Prayer:

Lord Jesus Christ, I believe You are the Son of the Living God and You took my sins on the cross and rose again from the dead. I trust You for forgiveness and the cleansing of my soul by Your precious blood from resentment, unforgiveness, offence and any activity I may have had in the occult. I come to You as my baptizer in the Holy Spirit. I yield my body to You and ask You to fill me and baptise me to make me fit for Your purposes in Your Kingdom, AMEN.

Now we are washed, sanctified and full of the Holy Spirit we can now enter into the Holy Place: A Place of Service unto God.

Chapter Four

THE HOLY PLACE
A PLACE OF SERVICE

"When they go into the Tabernacle of meeting, or when they come near the altar to minister, to burn an offering made by fire to the Lord, they shall wash with water, lest they die. So they shall wash their hands and their feet, lest they die." **Exodus 30:20-21** .

Now you are clean to serve a Holy God – This signifies that you are serious about being obedient to God. Previously, when we discussed the role and dress of the priesthood we learned that they had to be dressed appropriately for their service in the Tabernacle. There was special material used for the robes, tunics and headdress etc…Today we also need to be dressed for service but in this New Testament dispensation, this comes from our hearts, it's an inward dress. Jesus also gives us a robe of righteousness, a garment of praise for when we feel weary; of course this is a spiritual blessing and an anointing from the Holy Spirit. (**Isaiah 61:10**)

As we go through the curtain into the **Holy Place or Inner Court** instantly the aroma of the sweet incense that is burning before the Lord continually, fills your nostrils. It is quieter here as the sound of the animals grow dimmer as we are entering into a very special place. It is also a step closer to the **Holy of Holies** where the presence of God dwells. It is just beyond the next veil. You can see that it is so close and yet so far away as no one was allowed in there except the High Priest and only once a year.

Here things have changed dramatically from the crowded **Outer Court** of noisy people, the stench of blood, burnt carcasses, and furniture of bronze to furnishings made from a combination of acacia wood and pure gold. When you step back you see an overall view of the furnishings and contents: there is gold, frankincense and probably myrrh which we know was given to Jesus at His birth, and the wood in my own opinion represents His cross. We clearly see Jesus represented in all the pieces of furniture and objects here. **The Holy Place** also speaks of Jesus' servanthood.

You will note that there are just three pieces of furniture in the Holy Place and if you cast your eyes to the left you will see **The Menorah** - (Golden lampstand) and on your right, opposite the Menorah is **The Table of Showbread.** Straight ahead in front of the curtain that separates **The Holy of Holies** is **The Golden Altar of Incense.**

The Menorah

The MENORAH which is also called the Golden Lampstand/Candlestick, was hammered out of one piece of pure gold. The oil that fueled the light of the Menorah was poured into the little bowls at the top of each branch.

Like The Bronze Laver, there were no specific instructions about the size of the menorah but the fact that it was fashioned out of one piece of pure gold would maybe have limited its size.

It has a central branch from which three branches extend on each side forming a total of seven branches. Seven lamps holding olive oil and wicks stood on top of the branches. Each branch looked like that of an almond tree containing buds, blossoms and flowers. The priests were instructed to keep the lamps burning continuously.

"The Lord said to Moses, 'Command the Israelites to bring you clear oil of pressed olives for the light so that the lamps may be kept burning continually. Outside the curtain of the Testimony in the Tent of Meeting, Aaron is to tend the lamps before the Lord from evening till morning, continually.'" **Leviticus 24:1-3** .

The lampstand was the only source of light in the Holy Place, so without it, the priests would have been moving around in the dark. The light shone upon **The Table of Showbread** and the **Altar of Incense** to enable the priests to fellowship with God and intercede on behalf of God's people.

Just as the lampstand was placed in God's dwelling place so that the priests could approach God, Jesus, the *"true light that gives light to every man"* **John 1:9** . came into the world so that man could see God and not live in spiritual darkness anymore. Jesus said, *"I am the light of the world. Whoever follows me will never walk in darkness, but will have the light of life."* John 8:1 . Again He said, *"I have come* *into the world as a light so that no one who believes in me should stay in darkness."* **John 12:46** .

We can see Jesus here as represented by the main branch of the lampstand, and we as believers are represented by the six branches (six being the number of man) that extend from the original branch. Altogether, the seven branches of the Menorah is the number of completeness in Bible theology.

Having believed, we are now living as *"children of light;"* **Ephesians 5:8** who draw our source of light from Jesus, the true light. Jesus calls us the *"light of the world"* and commands us to *"let your light shine before men, that they may see your good deeds and praise your Father in heaven"* **Matthew 5:14-16** . The branches serve as a picture of Jesus' description of our relationship with him: *"I am the vine, you are the branches … apart from me you can do nothing"* **John 15:5** .

Two other significant symbols that can be seen include the fact that it was made of pure gold (not gold plated) and had seven branches. Pure gold is a representation of the deity and perfection of Jesus Christ, the gold was beaten, a type of Christ's suffering. There are buds, flowers and bowls that symbolises Christ's divine fruitfulness and availability to us.

FYI: Did you know that about 2200 years ago, Israel came under the rule of the Syrian-Greek emperor Antiochus, who issued many decrees designed to force his Hellenistic[1] ideology and

---
1. The Golden Age of Greek learning, Empire.

rituals upon the Jewish people? He outlawed the study of the Torah and its commands, and defiled the Holy Temple in Jerusalem with Greek idols.

A small, greatly outnumbered band of Jews led by Judean Macobeans battled against the mighty Greek armies, and drove them out of the land. When they reclaimed the Holy Temple, on the 25th of Kislev, they wanted to light the Temple's Menorah, only to find that the Greeks had contaminated virtually all the oil. All that remained was one cruse[2] of pure oil, enough to last one night and it would take eight days to procure new, pure oil.

Miraculously, the one-day supply of oil lasted eight days and nights, and the holiday of Hanukkah/Chanukah was established to commemorate and publicise these miracles. The Hanukkah/Chanukah menorah is lit on each of the eight nights of this festival of thanksgiving and memorial.

The Table of Shewbread

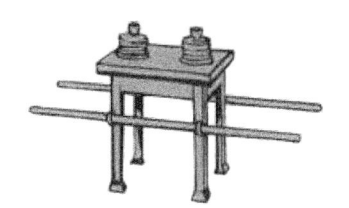

Now, let's walk across to **The Table of Shewbread or Table of Presence.**

The purpose of this golden table was to hold 12 cakes of bread made of fine flour. They were placed there in two rows of six,

---

2. A small vessel (such as a jar or pot) for holding a liquid (such as water or oil).
https://www.merriam-webster.com/dictionary/cruse

each loaf representing one of the tribes of Israel (**Lev. 24:8**).

"And you shall take fine flour and bake twelve cakes with it. Two-tenths of an ephah shall be in each cake. You shall set them in two rows, six in a row, on the pure gold table before the LORD. And you shall put pure frankincense on each row that it may be on the bread for a memorial, an offering made by fire to the LORD. Every Sabbath he shall set it in order before the LORD continually, being taken from the children of Israel by an everlasting covenant. And it shall be for Aaron and his sons, and they shall eat it in a holy place; for it is most holy to him from the offerings of the LORD made by fire, by a perpetual statute." **Lev 24:5-9**

God told Moses to put the Bread of the Presence on this table that it might be before Him at all times. Every seventh (Sabbath) day, fresh hot loaves were provided by Aaron the High Priest. The priests were entitled to eat the old loaves while standing in the Holy Place but they would find that the old bread always tasted as fresh as the day they were baked.

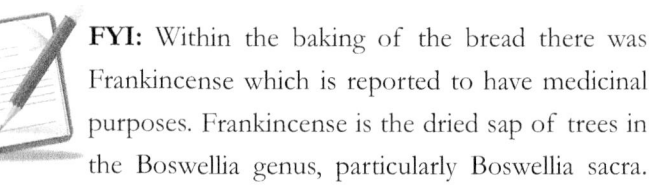

FYI: Within the baking of the bread there was Frankincense which is reported to have medicinal purposes. Frankincense is the dried sap of trees in the Boswellia genus, particularly Boswellia sacra. These trees grow in Oman, Yemen and the Horn of Africa, including Somalia and Ethiopia. When dried, the sap is burned as incense and thought to have several medicinal properties.[3]

---

3. https://www.livescience.com/25670-what-is-frankincense.
html#:~:text=Frankincense%20is%20the%20dried%20sap,to%20have%20several%20
medicinal%20properties.

It is wonderful how God took care of His priests. God knows how to keep His ministering priests healthy in a dry and barren place such as the wilderness.

Now we can begin to understand the words Jesus spoke in **John 6:48-5,** when He said, *"I am the bread of life. Your fathers ate the manna in the wilderness, and are dead. This is the bread which comes down from heaven that one may eat of it and not die. I AM the living bread which came down from heaven. If anyone eats of this bread, he will live forever; and the bread that I shall give is My flesh, which I shall give for the life of the world."*

As the shewbread was continually before God in the Holy Place so Jesus, the Bread of Life, is now seated at the right hand of God FOREVER INTERCEDING for us. For Christ has not entered the holy places made with hands, which are copies of the true, but into heaven itself, now to appear in the presence of God for us; **Hebrews 9:24** .

Jesus taught us in the Lord's Prayer to ask God the Father to, *"give us this day our daily Bread"* and for us this is the Word of God. In John's Gospel, Jesus is also identified as THE WORD, so feeding on THE WORD is the same as feeding on Christ.

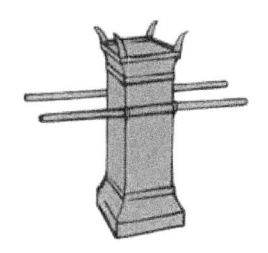

The Table of Incense

The Table Of Incense/The Golden Altar, is a special piece of furniture standing just in front of the veil that led to the Holy of Holies.

"You shall make an altar to burn incense on; you shall make it of acacia wood. A cubit shall be its length and a cubit its width, it shall be square, and two cubits shall be its height. Its horns shall be of one piece with it. And you shall overlay its top, its sides all around, and its horns with pure gold; and you shall make for it a moulding of gold all around. Two gold rings you shall make for it, under the moulding on both its sides. You shall place them on its two sides, and they will be holders for the poles with which to bear it. You shall make the poles of acacia wood, and overlay them with gold. And you shall put it before the veil that is before the ark of the Testimony, before the mercy seat that is over the Testimony, where I will meet with you…" **Exodus 30:1-10** .

The Golden Altar was used for burning incense that would be offered by Aaron the High Priest early in the morning and at twilight. The incense was lit twice every day by the priests after they had tended the wick and oil on the holy lamps. There were four horns on this altar, one on each edge. Its horns were also to be sprinkled with the blood from the sin offering. It is here that prayer was offered and if there was a breeze it would carry the fragrance outside of the tabernacle and the people would know that prayers were being offered continually.

In **Revelations 8:3-4** . an angel had a golden censer with much incense in it that he would offer it with the prayers of the saints and these ascended before God from the angel's hands. The incense that was burned on the altar of the tabernacle represents for Christians today the sweet smelling fragrance unto God that is our prayer and worship. God loves it when we seek Him, talk with Him and sing songs of adoration to Him. In **1 Thessalonians 5:7** . Paul, the apostle, says we should *"pray without ceasing."* As you can see, praying daily began first in the Tabernacle.

God gave the recipe for making the incense and stipulated that no other incense was ever to be burned on the altar (**Exodus 30:34-38**). The fire used to burn the incense was always taken from the altar of burnt offering outside the sanctuary (**Leviticus 16:12**). Never was the altar of incense to be used for any other kind of offering such as drink offerings etc. (**Exodus 30:9**). Once a year, on the Day of Atonement, the high priest was to put blood on the horns of the altar of incense to cleanse it. The altar of incense was said to be "most holy to the Lord" (**Exodus 30:10**).

So the LORD said to Moses, *"Take sweet spices, stacte and onycha and galbanum, and pure frankincense with these sweet spices; there shall be equal amounts of each. You shall make of these an incense, a compound according to the art of the perfumer, salted, pure, and holy. And you shall beat some of it very fine, and put some of it before the Testimony in the tabernacle of meeting where I will meet with you. It shall be most holy to you. But as for the incense which you shall make, you shall not make any for yourselves, according to its composition. It shall be to you holy for the LORD. Whoever makes any like it, to smell it, he shall be cut off from his people."* **Ex 30:34-38** .

So here in the Holy Place you will also notice there are no chairs to sit on; even when eating the priests could not sit down. Notice that everything is pointing to Jesus. How far removed today is the

Christian Church from this pattern that God has designed? We need to return the focus onto JESUS in our worship today.

The Tabernacle shows us Jesus the One who is the way to the only true God who alone can give eternal life. That is so clear here in The Holy Place. You can imagine that the sweet smell of the incense blotted out the stench of the slaughtered animals and so the fragrance of the Holy Place would have been wonderful compared to The Outer Court. The priests would also have this fragrance on them too. Similarly, when we serve and worship Jesus we too should carry the fragrance of Jesus' presence with us out into the world so that unbelievers will recognise the difference in us that Jesus makes.

The Showbread is Jesus/The Bread of Life - *"I am the bread of life. Your fathers ate the manna in the wilderness, and are dead. This is the bread which comes down from heaven that one may eat of it and not die. I am the living bread which came down from heaven. If anyone eats of this bread, he will live forever; and the bread that I shall give is My flesh, which I shall give for the life of the world."* **John 6:48-51**.

The Menorah is Jesus/The light of the World - Then Jesus spoke to them again, saying, *"I am the light of the world. He who follows Me shall not walk in darkness, but have the light of life."* **John 8:12**.

The incense is Jesus/The Anointed One - To the Son He says: *"Your throne, O God, is forever and ever; sceptre of righteousness is the sceptre of Your kingdom. You have loved righteousness and hated* *lawlessness; Therefore God, Your God, has anointed You With the oil of gladness more than Your companions."* **Hebrews 1:8-9**

The Holy Place is a place of servant hood 24/7 and here we see that God has provided all we need to serve Him. Food, warmth, light and health. I could share so many testimonies of how the Lord Jesus has provided for me and my family as we have put our faith and trust in Him. Even during financial hardship He provided and we never went hungry. Someone would always turn up with food at the right time.

My body has been subjected to many illnesses which He has cured.[4]

"And every priest stands ministering daily and offering repeatedly the same sacrifices, which can never take away sins. But this Man (Jesus) after He had offered one sacrifice for sins forever, sat down at the right hand of God, from that time waiting till His enemies are made His footstool. For by one offering He has perfected forever those who are being sanctified." **Heb 10:11-14** .

Do you remember that the gold, frankincense and myrrh found in The Holy Place was also brought by the Wise men and presented to Jesus at His birth in Bethlehem?

---

[4]. You can read of some of these in my book REACH FOR YOUR MIRACLE available on Amazon

Notes

Chapter Five

THE MOST HOLY PLACE
A PLACE OF SURRENDER

"You shall make a veil woven of blue, purple, and scarlet thread, and fine woven linen. And you shall hang the veil from the clasps. Then you shall bring the ark of the Testimony in there, behind the veil. The veil shall be a divider for you between the Holy place and the Most Holy; it shall be woven with an artistic design of cherubim." **Exodus 26:31** .

At the beginning our aim was to approach the Holy God of Israel and this is the place our tour ends and yet, this is also the place where a deeper spiritual journey can begin. This is where we encounter God: You and God alone in the most sacred and holiest place in the Tabernacle. We have reached our destination but is it the end or just another beginning?

Notice that here only a linen curtain or veil hangs between The Holy Place and The Most Holy Place/Holy of Holies. As you stand here you can be lost in the moment, you can see the shadow of the Ark of the Covenant through that veil. You desperately want to go into the Holy of Holies and meet with God, after all isn't this why you took this journey?

Your hands start to tremble, your whole being is filled with excitement and yet in fear, wonder and apprehension you still reach out. The only obstacle in your way is a veil and of course as you touch it you are immediately transported from The Holy Place to the Holy of Holies (figuratively speaking).

The veil itself is a sacred furnishing, if you remember, everything in the Tabernacle was sanctified by God through the sprinkling of blood sacrifice at the completion of the Tabernacle. Here at last is where God promised to meet with Moses and Aaron, in a cloud, at the Mercy Seat of the Ark of the Covenant. (**Leviticus 16:2**)

The quietness and the peace that now floods your soul are unimaginable. What can you do except kneel before a Holy God? This is no longer a place, just for the High Priest. This intimacy is no longer just for Israel, this is for the whole world thanks to Jesus' blood on the Mercy Seat in Heaven.

As we bow in reverence we sense the love that God has for us, we sense His joy at our coming to Him, but above all our wanting to come to Him. Our desire to have an intimate relationship with Him has been so strong that we were prepared to go through 'the stages' of the Tabernacle for this very precious moment.

Today the veil no one was even allowed to touch in the wilderness has been ripped in two indicating an opening for us all to enter The Holy of Holies. We can all now experience the presence and glory of the Lord in The Holy of Holies where once only the High Priest could go. There is a condition of course for this wonderful privilege of meeting with God and that is, we need to accept that Jesus suffered and died for our sins; that He and He only has made a way through the veil. For those of us who have done this and believe in the Lord, we no longer look through a veil dimly, now we have access to that Holiest Place to meet with Him face to face.

The Ark of the Covenant

The Ark of the Covenant (Atonement cover AT/ONE/MENT God at one with man)

The Ark of the Covenant was simply a man made wooden chest overlaid with gold as instructed by God through Moses that represented God's judgement, mercy, presence and throne of authority. As I mentioned earlier, gold also depicts Deity.

Only the High priest could enter through the veil into **The Holy Of Holies** with the blood of animals that had been sacrificed and that only once a year on the Day of Atonement (10th day of the 7th month in the Hebrew calendar is the month of Tishri, Sept/Oct)

No one else could be in the Tabernacle whilst the High Priest was making atonement for sin. He stood alone. Then he would sprinkle the blood of the animals on **The Mercy Seat of the Ark of the Covenant** as if to say, Yahweh (Hebrew) have mercy on us!

The Mercy Seat, also covered in Gold, has two cherubim forms of protective angels with wings covering the seat. On the Mercy Seat the blood of sacrifice was sprinkled by the High Priest for the atonement of sin. The mercy seat is where our sins are forgiven and removed. The place where we are reconciled to God.

The only piece of furniture in the Holy of Holies is the Ark of the Covenant. If we were to open it and take a look inside we would see that it contained:
1. Aaron's Budded Rod (**Numbers 17**)
2. The Ten Commandments (**Exodus 20**)
3. A Gold pot containing Manna (**Exodus 16: 33**)

The Ten Commandments represented the law, the pot of manna represented God's sustenance and the budded rod of Aaron's staff represented the sovereignty of God. He over-rules all others, He has the final say.

Now the Mercy seat was a lid above the Covenant box that covered the Law and also the cloud of the glory of God (Shekinah in Hebrew) showing His presence (**Leviticus 16**).

This also represented God's presence amongst His people and some of the major miracles He performed during their journey. He has always desired to dwell among His people. Moses had said to the Lord, if your presence does not go with us do not send us up from here. **Exodus: 33:12–15** . God showed Moses and the people His presence by a cloud going before them by day and fire before them at night. There are numerous accounts of the great exodus from Egypt and their 40 year journey, which should have only taken them 11 days by the way, but God was preparing them for the Promised Land and so it took longer than 11 days. As with us God is preparing us for our Heavenly home.

"But when the kindness and the love of God our Saviour toward man appeared, not by works of righteousness (law) which we have done, but according to His mercy He saved us, through the washing of regeneration and renewing of the Holy Spirit" **Titus 3:4-5** .

After Jesus died on the cross, where He shed His blood for our sins, He went into the Heavenly Tabernacle and presented His blood to the Father FOR THE WHOLE WORLD… JEW AND GENTILE… Once and for all time.

So what has changed that enabled those of us who believe in Jesus to enter The Holy of Holies?
The Jerusalem temple, built by Solomon, is a replica of the wilderness tabernacle; only this had a curtain/veil that was about 60 feet in height, 30 feet in width and four inches thick.

As Jesus cried out in victory, "IT IS FINISHED" it was torn from top down, meaning this could only have been God's doing. As the veil was torn, The Holy of Holies was now exposed; a way was made for the world to be reconciled to God through the death and resurrection of Jesus Christ (Yeshua in Hebrew).

The temple on Earth in physical Jerusalem has been destroyed leaving only remnants of its foundation on the temple mount and the western wall, that is now under Muslim occupation. However, there is of course a Heavenly Temple or Tabernacle and this is the one we can look forward to.

"Then the temple of God was opened in heaven, and the Ark of His covenant was seen in His temple. And there were lightning, noises, thundering, an earthquake, and great hail" **Revelations 11:19** . There is no veil there either, as Jesus has eternally removed all barriers to us having access to God. What a wonderful journey we have taken through the Tabernacle and, believe it or not, there is so much more we could learn from the furnishings or of the precious metals but maybe your appetite for more will lead you to read for yourself.

I pray you have enjoyed the tour through the Tabernacle and clearly seen Jesus the Messiah within it. Every blessing.

WHERE ARE YOU WITH YOUR WALK WITH GOD?

```
HOLY OF HOLIES
Surrender
---------------------------
HOLY PLACE
Service
---------------------------
OUTER COURT
Sanctification
Sacrifice For Sin
```

FYI-603,550 PEOPLE OF THE 12 TRIBES OF ISRAEL

HAD NO ACCESS TO GOD ONLY THOSE WHO WERE MEMBERS OF THE PRIESTHOOD

A Better Way

God went through a lot of time, trouble, heartache and joy to dwell with His people even to the sacrificing of His own Son to show how serious His covenant with us is. For Eternal Life. So we need to acknowledge that today and begin to spend quality time dwelling in His presence. **Hebrews 4:4 – 5:1 -9** .

For Christ did not enter a Holy place made with hands, a [mere] copy of the true one, but into heaven itself, now to appear in the presence of God for us… **Hebrews 9:24** .

This gradual approach towards God starts with an acknowledgement of sin and bringing a sacrifice that would be acceptable for the priests to slaughter ceremoniously and they would go away and hope that God had forgiven them.

Today, it is when we acknowledge our sin before a Holy God and accept that the price and penalty for sin has been dealt with and when we surrender our hearts and lives to Jesus; we do not go away hoping He will forgive us. We go away knowing He HAS FORGIVEN US.

We have Jesus with us all the time by His Holy Spirit helping us on our journey to everlasting life, setting us free from the law of sin and death and obtaining His Mercy. He is waiting to welcome us in our eternal home in HEAVEN. JESUS said, *"I have come to give you life and that more abundantly."* John 10:10

WHAT ARE YOU WAITING FOR? IT IS DONE IT IS FINISHED!

Notes